EXTREME SURVIVAL

MILITARY SURVIVAL

Nick Hunter

Raintree
Chicago, Illinois

www.heinemannraintree.com
Visit our website to find out more information about Heinemann-Raintree books.

To order:
☎ Phone 888-454-2279
Visit www.heinemannraintree.com to browse our catalog and order online.

Edited by Adam Miller, Adrian Vigliano, and Andrew Farrow
Designed by Steve Mead
Original illustrations © Capstone Global Library Ltd.
Illustrated by Jeff Edwards and KJA-Artists.com
Picture research by Tracy Cummins
Production by Camilla Crask
Originated by Capstone Global Library Ltd
Printed and bound in the United States of America, North Mankato, MN

15 14 13 12 11
10 9 8 7 6 5 4 3 2 1

Library of Congress Cataloging-in-Publication Data
Hunter, Nick.
  Military survival / Nick Hunter.
    p. cm.—(Extreme survival)
  Includes bibliographical references and index.
  ISBN 978-1-4109-3970-8 (hc)
  ISBN 978-1-4109-3977-7 (pb)
  1. Survival skills—Juvenile literature. 2. Combat survival—Juvenile literature. I. Title.
  U225.H86 2011
  613.6—dc22   2010028837

Acknowledgments
The author and publishers are grateful to the following for permission to reproduce copyright material: AP Photo p. **12** (Australian Defense Department/CPL Bernard Pearson, HO); Corbis pp. **26** (©Alain Nogues/Sygma), **32** (©Corbis), **46** (©Helmiy al-Azawi/Reuters), **27** (©Jeffrey Markowitz), **42** (©Peter Turnley); DefenseImagery.com pp. **8** (AMN CHRISTOPHER), **4 & 5** (SPC Harold Field), **40** (SPC Jackson), **31** (TSgt. Scott P. Stewart); Getty Images pp. **19**, **36** (AFP), **49** (AFP Massoud Hossaini), **47** (AFP/Murray Wray), **23** top (Ali Yussef/AFP), **38** (Ami Vitale), **25 & 35** (Keystone), **45** (Popperfoto), **20** (Scott Peterson), **14** (STF), **11** (Tim Turner/U.S. Navy), **13** (Tom Weber/MIL pictures); Rex USA p. **17** bottom; Shutterstock p. **17** top (©Testing); U.S. Air Force pp. **6** (Dennis Rogers), **23** bottom (SrA Kenny Holston), **28** (Tech. Sgt. Francisco V. Govea II); World Picture News p. **15** (Andrew Chittock).

Cover photograph reproduced with the permission of Getty Images/Tyler Stableford. Cover background image reproduced with the permission of istockphoto/© clearviewimages.

We would like to thank Ann Fullick for her invaluable help in the preparation of this book.

Every effort has been made to contact copyright holders of any material reproduced in this book. Any omissions will be rectified in subsequent printings if notice is given to the publisher.

Disclaimer
All the Internet addresses (URLs) given in this book were valid at the time of going to press. However, due to the dynamic nature of the Internet, some addresses may have changed, or sites may have changed or ceased to exist since publication. While the author and publisher regret any inconvenience this may cause readers, no responsibility for any such changes can be accepted by either the author or the publisher.

CONTENTS

Some words are printed in bold, **like this**. You can find out what they mean by looking in the glossary.

EXTREME SURVIVAL

In late September 2001, rumors circulated that U.S. Delta Force and British Special Air Service troops were gathering information and identifying targets in Afghanistan. They seemed to be preparing for an invasion. These **special forces** develop amazing survival skills through years of tough training and combat experience. They are trained to work behind enemy lines in small units, surviving in harsh conditions.

The U.S. and British governments would not comment on the rumors. Special forces missions are secret. But then, on October 7, 2001, cruise missiles were launched from submarines and surface ships in the Arabian Sea, and planes began bombing runs. They attacked many targets that the special forces had identified. This was the start of a conflict that would last for many years.

Surviving conflicts

This book looks at some of the greatest stories of military courage and survival, from World War I to recent conflicts in Iraq and Afghanistan. It will examine how soldiers are trained to survive in **hostile** territory under mental and physical stress. It will look at basic survival techniques, as well as how soldiers deal with capture and escape. The book will also consider the stories of people who have been caught up in conflict and found a way to survive.

People in the military today are sometimes placed in life-threatening situations. What are the special qualities that pull them through when survival seems impossible? A later chapter will ask you to consider how you would react in some of these situations. Would you survive?

"'The Will to Live' means never giving in, regardless of the situation. It's very reassuring to know that there is nothing on this Earth that we cannot deal with, and there is no place where we cannot survive. As long as we follow the basic survival principles, prepare ourselves, and apply this 'Will to Live,' we will come through." —John "Lofty" Wiseman, former British Special Air Service officer

Soldiers of the U.S.-led force in Afghanistan need all their survival skills in the harsh mountain environment.

TRAINING TO SURVIVE

In an increasingly unstable world, those who join the armed forces—like the army, navy, and air force—need to be able to fight and survive in a huge range of situations. Basic training gives new **recruits** the main skills they will need to survive. It is designed to turn everyday people, or **civilians**, into soldiers. After a short period of basic training, recruits receive more detailed training in a specialized area.

Physical training

Physical fitness is a basic requirement for military survival. Imagine having to march many miles carrying a heavy backpack and weapons, while also wearing bulky body armor. Or imagine the concentration needed to fly regular missions in a supersonic jet fighter.

Both situations depend on being physically fit and eating a balanced diet. Fitness training for recruits will include exercises to build up strength, such as push-ups, as well as running and marching with heavy equipment. These exercises help to build up strength and **endurance**, or the ability to keep going. Obstacle courses are another important part of military physical training.

Assault courses build strength and sharpen soldiers' skills in moving across a range of different **terrains** and obstacles. One day these skills may mean the difference between escape and capture.

Mental toughness

Survival in a combat situation often depends on quick thinking and clear decisions. Mental toughness allows soldiers to avoid any small mistake that could lead them into danger. Military training aims to build up the mental strength necessary to survive. Tough discipline ensures that recruits learn to avoid mistakes and to work well under stress.

Recruits are also taught to work as a team. In the heat of a battle or in a survival situation, each member of the team needs to know his or her role and be able to work well with others. Again, discipline is essential. Leadership and following orders are very important and could mean the difference between life and death.

U.S. ARMY PHYSICAL FITNESS TRAINING

Soldiers are tested regularly for physical fitness. U.S. soldiers take a physical fitness test every six months to ensure they are fit enough. The standards vary depending on age, but the minimum requirements for those between 17 and 21 years old are as follows:

	Push-ups	Sit-ups	Time for running 2 miles
Male	42	53	15 min., 54 sec.
Female	19	53	18 min., 54 sec.

BRITISH ARMY PHYSICAL STANDARDS

Military personnel are tested regularly for physical fitness. Standards vary slightly across the British Army. Standards for officer recruits are as follows:

	Push-ups in 2 minutes	Sit-ups in 2 minutes	Running*
Male	44	50	1.5 miles in 10.5 minutes
Female	21	50	1.5 miles in 13 minutes

* The running test is the equivalent of 2.4 kilometers (1.5 miles), completed by running shuttles over a 20-meter track.

Source: British Army website (www.army.mod.uk)

Surviving in the field

A recruit could be fighting overseas the day after his or her training finishes. The experience gained during survival training will bring the confidence to deal with any real situation.

SERE training: Survival and Evasion

SERE stands for "Survival, **Evasion**, Resistance, and Escape." This kind of training is designed to prepare recruits for surviving in a **hostile** environment, where capture by the enemy is a real possibility. General survival skills are important, such as finding food and water.

This training also focuses on evasion, or the planning needed to avoid capture. This includes **camouflage**, building a concealed shelter, and moving without being detected.

Soldiers are taught to travel at night or during bad weather and not to leave tracks. Soldiers must also figure out the best way to get back to friendly territory, which often means **navigating** out of enemy territory. Soldiers learn how to navigate without a compass and also how to signal to rescuers. (See pages 28 and 29 for more on surviving behind enemy lines.)

SERE training prepares soldiers for what will happen if they are captured. According to the Geneva Conventions (see page 34), prisoners only need to give their name, rank and serial number. However, some captors will do all they can to get more information.

SERE training: Resistance and Escape

The most difficult aspect of SERE training is dealing with being captured. Soldiers will go through exercises about what to do when captured, including how to behave toward captors. (See pages 34 to 37 for more information on prisoners of war.) This training is secret and based on the experience of prisoners in previous conflicts.

The U.S. military Code of Conduct states that captives should "make every effort to escape and to aid others to escape." This is the final part of SERE training. Escaping and evading recapture is very difficult. There are some stories of heroic escapes and rescues later in this book.

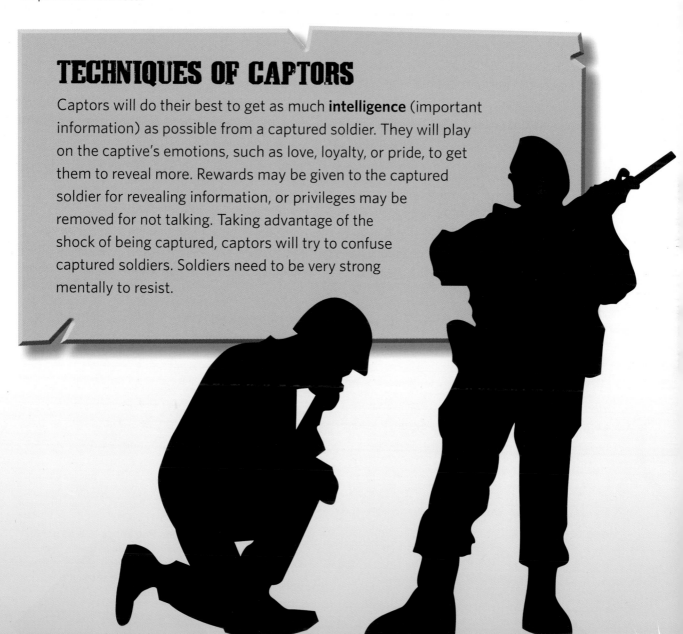

TECHNIQUES OF CAPTORS

Captors will do their best to get as much **intelligence** (important information) as possible from a captured soldier. They will play on the captive's emotions, such as love, loyalty, or pride, to get them to reveal more. Rewards may be given to the captured soldier for revealing information, or privileges may be removed for not talking. Taking advantage of the shock of being captured, captors will try to confuse captured soldiers. Soldiers need to be very strong mentally to resist.

SPECIAL FORCES

As darkness fell on June 27, 2005, a unit of four **special forces** soldiers, called Navy SEALs, left their base in Afghanistan to assist a mission to capture a leader of the enemy, the Taliban. The Taliban was the former government of Afghanistan, which had supported **terrorist** groups. The SEAL team's mission was to establish the leader's location so he could be captured. Dropped from a helicopter in enemy territory, the Navy SEALs trekked across rugged mountainsides, before taking up position watching a village, where they believed the target was. After being accidentally discovered by three Afghan farmers, they were suddenly attacked by a large force of Taliban fighters.

Three of the four SEALs were killed in the battle that followed. A helicopter carrying a rescue team was also shot down, killing all onboard. Lead Petty Officer Marcus Luttrell was the sole survivor, after being blown down the mountain by a grenade. Luttrell had an injured back and leg and had lost most of his equipment, including his pants. And he was still being pursued by the Taliban. As he wrote in his account of the mission: "Every decision I made from now on would involve my own life and death. I needed to fight my way out."

Surviving against all odds

Luttrell's main problem in the dry mountains, apart from the enemy, was thirst. The human body can survive for many days without food, but not for long without water. He tried breaking and sucking branches and grasses to get a few drops of water. Eventually, almost overcome by thirst, he heard a mountain stream. But before he could reach it, he was attacked again by the Taliban and shot in the leg. Eventually, Luttrell reached the stream, only to discover that he was being watched by three armed Afghans. They took him to their village, cared for his wounds, and refused to hand him over to the Taliban, risking the safety of their whole village.

After several days, one of the villagers, carrying a letter from Luttrell, managed to make his way to a Marine outpost. This allowed U.S. soldiers to determine Luttrell's location and eventually rescue him. As this story of Operation Red Wings shows, special forces soldiers must learn how to survive in the most extreme circumstances.

The story of Operation Red Wings tells us not just about the survival skills of special forces in the most extreme circumstances, but also that Officer Luttrell would not have survived without the support of the local people.

Special forces troops use light armored vehicles for patrolling enemy territory. These Australian special forces commandos are in Afghanistan.

History of special forces

Members of the special forces, like Officer Luttrell, are an **elite** group. They are specially selected to be the best and most highly trained soldiers. They generally operate in small groups, behind enemy lines. The special forces units established during World War II (1939–45) helped create the model for today's special forces. One of the first and most influential was the British Special Air Service, which formed in North Africa in 1941. U.S. Army Special Forces were established in 1952, and since then special forces operations have become increasingly important in modern warfare. Many other nations have established their own special forces units, including Australia, New Zealand, and Germany.

U.S. special operations

In the early 2000s, around 50,000 troops were involved in U.S. special operations. These included the Green Berets, who specialize in helping other nations fight against terrorists and other common enemies. Army Rangers are soldiers trained to capture and secure key positions. Navy SEALs (short for "Sea, Air, and Land"), like Officer Luttrell, are the U.S. Navy's special operations troops. The secretive Delta Force mainly deals with the threat of terrorists.

Selection and training

The selection process and training required to join special forces are very tough. Many applicants do not make it through the initial assessment classes. Special forces **recruits** undergo several areas of training before qualification, including **SERE training** and classes in which they learn how to **navigate**. Extensive field exercises help prepare soldiers for the unexpected. Training for the special forces needs to give these troops the best possible chance of surviving and completing their missions.

It is a basic requirement for all special forces soldiers to speak a foreign language, such as Russian, Arabic, Chinese, or Spanish. The ability to adapt to local cultures is also essential for survival—another lesson learned by Officer Luttrell's ordeal, when he was helped by local Afghan citizens.

Heavy **camouflage** helps these Green Berets stay hidden. Walking through water will cover their tracks.

The Special Air Service

One of the world's best-known special forces is the British Special Air Service, or SAS. The SAS became famous around the world after the daring rescue of **hostages** from the Iranian **Embassy** (official headquarters) in London in 1980. It became known for having the toughest training in the British Army.

THE SAS FOUR–MAN PATROL

The basic unit of the SAS is the four-man patrol. This unit combines the firepower and expertise needed to carry out SAS operations. Each group includes a signaler, demolitions (explosives) expert, medical specialist, and languages expert. Each member has enough knowledge of each of these skills to fill in if another specialist is killed.

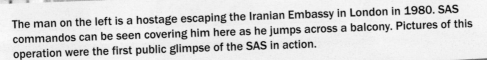

The man on the left is a hostage escaping the Iranian Embassy in London in 1980. SAS commandos can be seen covering him here as he jumps across a balcony. Pictures of this operation were the first public glimpse of the SAS in action.

Recruiting and training the best

SAS members all have experience in other areas of the military. The selection process begins with one month of training in the Brecon Beacons Mountains in Wales. This training is designed to find those who have the **endurance** and mental strength to join the regiment. In the "Long Drag," volunteers have to navigate on their own for 64 kilometers (40 miles) in under 24 hours, carrying a 25-kilogram (55-pound) backpack. After this, the recruits train extensively to become part of a standard four-man SAS operating unit. This is followed by jungle and parachute training.

After training, SAS soldiers are expected to be resourceful, mentally and physically fit, and able to work in small units for long periods without support. They are expected to keep a cool head at all times.

SAS operations

During the Falklands War of 1982, the United Kingdom fought Argentina over the control of islands off South America. The SAS demonstrated their survival skills during this conflict. Dropped by helicopter onto the islands, they survived for weeks in hiding in the cold, harsh **climate**. They provided **intelligence** on Argentine forces and destroyed aircraft and other targets on the ground.

In 2003 the survival skills of British special forces were also put to the test in the Iraq War (2003–present), when they fought alongside the United States. Special Boat Service (SBS) soldiers, the Royal Navy equivalent of the SAS, were suddenly attacked by Iraqi soldiers. Eight members of the patrol were able to escape into the hills and send a signal to be picked up by helicopter. Two members of the patrol set off for the Syrian border. Traveling at night to avoid being seen, they crept through an area with many Iraqi patrols and then across empty desert, before finally reaching safety.

These soldiers are in training in the Brecon Beacons Mountains in Wales. Their goal is to join the SAS after training.

Bravo Two Zero

Even the most highly trained soldiers can sometimes come up against impossible survival challenges. During the Gulf War (1990–91), three SAS units were sent to patrol main routes in Iraq. Two of the patrols quickly realized that the desert landscape would offer little cover, so they ended the mission. But the third patrol, called B20 or Bravo Two Zero, would have its survival skills tested to the absolute limit.

The eight-man patrol was expected to carry all its food and equipment for two weeks. The soldiers were dropped into Iraq carrying backpacks weighing 75 kilograms (165 pounds). Attacked by Iraqi forces, the soldiers were forced to dump their heavy backpacks, which left them with only the bare minimum they needed to survive. They knew that their best hope was to reach the border of Syria, a long march to the north (see the map below).

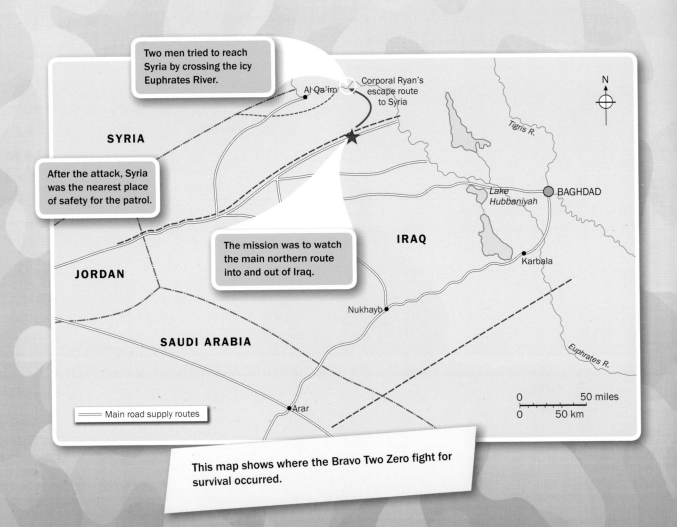

Two men tried to reach Syria by crossing the icy Euphrates River.

Corporal Ryan's escape route to Syria

After the attack, Syria was the nearest place of safety for the patrol.

The mission was to watch the main northern route into and out of Iraq.

Main road supply routes

0   50 miles
0   50 km

This map shows where the Bravo Two Zero fight for survival occurred.

NAVIGATION

A compass is an essential piece of survival equipment. But without a compass, the stars can be used for navigation. In the Northern Hemisphere—which includes Europe, North America, most of Asia, parts of Africa, and a small part of South America—the North or Pole Star will show where north is. In the Southern Hemisphere—which includes Antarctica, Australia, parts of Africa, and most of South America—the South Pole can be located by looking for the Southern Cross **constellation** (group of stars).

Surviving alone

In freezing winter weather, three members of the team became separated from the rest. The remaining group of five men got close to the Syrian border, but ran into an Iraqi patrol. Two men were captured and another man was killed. The remaining two members of this group swam across the wide, icy waters of the Euphrates River. One man died from **hypothermia** (loss of body heat), and the other was captured getting help.

Meanwhile, the three separated members of the group struggled to survive. One died from hypothermia and exhaustion. Another was captured when he asked Iraqi **civilians** for help. Corporal "Chris Ryan" (not his real name) was the only member of the patrol left who could make it to safety. Using only a compass, Ryan walked more than 160 kilometers (100 miles) to the Syrian border. His only food for a week was two packages of cookies. Once he crossed the border into Syria, Ryan was given food and water by a local man, and he was eventually able to make contact with the British embassy.

There were a number of different accounts of the mission. As always, official government sources refuse to comment on special forces operations.

Sergeant Vincent Phillips of Bravo Two Zero. Sergeant Phillips was one of the three group members who were separated from the main unit. He died of hypothermia while trying to reach the Syrian border.

UNDER FIRE

As dawn broke over the coast of northern France on June 6, 1944 (later known as D-Day), more than 100,000 men landed on the beaches of Normandy. The aim of this force from many nations—known as the Allies, and including the United States, United Kingdom, and Canada—was to attack the German defenses on the coast and begin the Allied invasion of Europe. As the landing craft neared the shore, the noise became deafening. Missiles, cannons, and machine guns roared from the beaches and from the huge fleet of ships supporting the invasion. At Omaha Beach, the U.S. 1st Infantrymen jumped from their landing craft under heavy fire, landing in water up to their chests.

Surviving D-Day

Soldiers were exposed to fire as they left their landing craft. Some ducked below the level of the water for as long as they could, so they would not be obvious targets. Others took shelter behind concrete obstacles on the beach. Many crawled to make themselves less visible as targets. Their focus was to reach the sea wall at the top of the beach, where they would have some protection.

Medics tried to stop the loss of blood for those who had been injured on the battlefield. Half of all military personnel killed in action die from loss of blood, and most of those in the first hour after being injured. The "first field dressing" is essential in saving lives.

SURVIVAL SCIENCE:

Battlefield medicine

By the end of August 1944, Allied troops had suffered more than 209,000 **casualties** (deaths and injuries). However, a U.S. soldier was half as likely to die from his injuries in World War II as in World War I (1914–18). Important medical breakthroughs saved lives, including medicines like penicillin and **antiseptics**, which prevented infection. Advances in blood transfusions, which transfer blood from one person to another, also saved many lives.

Stopping loss of blood was a crucial part of treating the wounded at D-Day and this has continued until the present day. Forces in Afghanistan have developed new dressings to treat victims of bomb blasts and these techniques have helped to save lives outside the military.

As soldiers jumped from landing craft on D-Day, their already heavy equipment became heavier as their clothes became soaked with water. Then, under fire, they had to quickly attack German defenses.

Blackhawk down in Somalia

Huge attacks such as the D-Day landings are rare in modern warfare. Today's troops are more likely to come under fire in small groups in **hostile** places.

In 1993 U.S. forces were serving in Mogadishu, Somalia, in Africa, alongside a **United Nations** mission. Their aim was to help food and supplies reach the starving people of Somalia. They were also working to bring peace to the region.

On October 3, Delta Force and Army Rangers set off on a dangerous mission. They were going to try to capture senior members of one of the warring clans (groups) causing unrest in the region. This meant going into an area of the city controlled by the clan. Since it was a city, the buildings surrounding the area made it difficult for both helicopters and vehicles to **navigate**.

U.S. soldiers in Somalia risked their lives to rescue the crews of the two Blackhawk helicopters brought down in the hostile city.

During the raid, a U.S. Blackhawk helicopter was shot down by enemy fire. The decision was made to rescue the crew onboard the fallen helicopter, even though they may have been killed in the crash. During the attempt, another helicopter crashed. Several missions were sent to try to rescue the fallen soldiers, but most were unable to reach the crash site in such hostile territory.

During this incident, 18 U.S. soldiers were killed. But there were some amazing tales of courage. Two Delta Force soldiers fought their way on foot through a heavily armed mob of people in an attempt to rescue the crew of the second helicopter. They were killed in the attempt.

Modern dangers

This incident shows many of the dangers of modern warfare. This battle was not fought on a battlefield, but rather in the crowded streets of a hostile city. It shows many of the things needed to survive. Helicopters were used to minimize casualties on the ground, but the crowded city landscape left them open to attack. The troops in the Somalia mission were working under a number of different commanders, from both the United Nations and the U.S. military. This led to confusion. In such a confusing situation, clear communication and clear goals are essential.

SURVIVAL SCIENCE

Reconstructing bodies and lives

Many of those who survive being wounded in conflict are left with severe problems for the rest of their lives, both physical and mental. Many soldiers suffer the loss of limbs. Fortunately, artificial limbs have developed enormously in recent years. The I-limb is a hand that has five moving fingers. It is controlled by a computer chip that detects signals from the survivor's arm muscles.

Modern challenges

The experience of U.S. troops in Somalia highlights some factors that are common to modern wars. Today, Western troops are rarely fighting against uniformed armies, as they were in the world wars. Sometimes the enemies they are fighting are dressed in the same clothes as the **civilian** population. This presents new challenges for survival. Soldiers must put lots of effort into getting the support of the local population (see box below).

HEARTS AND MINDS

Special forces are often operating in secret behind enemy lines. For example, Australian special forces in Afghanistan went out of their way to build trust, having tea with local elders and emphasizing that they had no issues with ordinary people. They were able to capture large quantities of weapons with the support of local people. Often, in a survival situation, the support and help of local people can mean the difference between life and death.

Terrain—or specific kinds of local land—can also be a major factor in modern warfare. The attempted rescue of the Blackhawk crews in Somalia took place in an unfamiliar city. A city is difficult terrain because it provides lots of ways for enemies to conceal themselves. Fighting in desert, mountain, or jungle conditions also require very different sets of survival skills (see pages 40 to 43).

Improvised Explosive Devices

Today's military patrols are just as likely to have to deal with small groups of fighters, called **guerrillas**, as an all-out assault from official combat troops. The **Improvised Explosive Device (IED)** has been a key weapon used by guerrilla forces in recent conflicts in Iraq and Afghanistan. IEDs are bombs made from everyday materials. They are often placed alongside roads.

Minefields are also common. These are areas where explosives are spread out, to be activated when people step on them. They are sometimes used to prevent enemies from using a certain path.

To survive in these conditions, armies have adapted. Both the United States and the United Kingdom have developed patrol vehicles that are more resistant to IEDs. Helicopters have also become much more important for transporting troops over rough and dangerous terrain, so as to avoid IEDs altogether.

BOMB DISPOSAL

IEDs have been responsible for many military and civilian deaths in Afghanistan. One of the most dangerous jobs in any army is defusing bombs, which means making them ineffective. Bomb disposal experts train for up to eight years and can defuse many bombs in a single night. Robots, such as the one in the picture at right, are used to identify and examine bombs, but only a highly trained human can make them safe.

Chinook helicopters are the safest way to carry troops and equipment in hostile areas, where minefields and IEDs are common.

SURVIVAL IN THE SKY

In the summer of 1940, during World War II, a battle to survive took place over southern England. As German fighter and bomber planes attacked Britain, Royal Air Force (RAF) pilots scrambled into their Spitfires and Hurricanes, determined to win the Battle of Britain. Their aim was to get to the same **altitude** (height) as the German attackers as quickly as possible. The RAF pilots could then engage the enemy in a "dogfight," meaning they could fight closely. Planes traveling at over 480 kilometers per hour (300 miles per hour) chased each other, firing machine guns as enemy planes flashed by.

Surviving the Battle of Britain

Pilots in the Battle of Britain were in constant danger. By the end of September 1940, most had been shot down at least once. If they were able to bail out in time, they stood a good chance of surviving, since they were fighting over friendly territory. Their planes were very cramped, with only a metal plate behind them and reinforced windshield to protect them. Pilots wore many layers of clothing for warmth, and also to guard against burns if they were hit. Plastic surgery was just developing, and was used to treat many unlucky burn victims.

Exhaustion was a major problem for the pilots. They were in action every day, and there was always the stress that they might not come back alive. There are stories of pilots falling asleep on their way back from missions. British Prime Minister Winston Churchill paid tribute to their courage and will to survive, saying, "Never in the field of human conflict, was so much owed by so many to so few."

SURVIVAL SCIENCE:

Exhaustion

Coping with lack of sleep is part of military training. The need to be alert means that sleep is often limited. Lack of sleep causes clumsiness and affects the brain's ability to make decisions. Although there are cases of people going without sleep for many days, it would be impossible to operate a complex fighter aircraft without regular sleep.

As soon as the pilots were told that enemy aircraft were on the way, they faced a race against time to get into the air quickly. The pilots would be less likely to survive a dogfight if they could not reach the same altitude as enemy aircraft.

SURVIVAL SCIENCE:

G-force

The bodies of jet fighter pilots are subject to extraordinary forces called **g-forces**. Our bodies are used to the force of **gravity**, which we experience on the surface of Earth. Gravity is the force that holds us down. Earth's gravity is defined as 1 g. However, fighter pilots can experience more than 9 g—for example, while making sharp turns. Ejecting from a jet fighter produces even higher g-forces. High g-forces cause the blood in pilots' bodies to rush to their feet and away from their brains. Special training and g-suits, which restrict the flow of blood, enable pilots to withstand these forces more easily. In extreme circumstances, high g-forces can cause G-LOC (Gravity-induced Loss of Consciousness) or even death.

A fighter pilot ejects from a speeding aircraft. Pilots will typically only use an ejection seat in an emergency. Many ejection seats subject pilots to higher g-forces than they experience while flying, not to mention other dangers, such as being shot at from enemies on the ground!

Shot down over Bosnia

If pilots are shot down behind enemy lines, they need to be ready to avoid capture and survive until they can be rescued. In 1995 Captain Scott O'Grady of the U.S. Air Force had to fight for survival when his F-16 fighter was shot down while he was on a mission over Bosnia, in southeastern Europe.

O'Grady was part of an international force preventing Serbian aircraft from flying in the region. Suddenly, his plane was hit by a missile. O'Grady ejected himself from his plane, exposing his body to the dangers of g-forces (see box at left). But that was just the beginning of his ordeal. He would have to survive six days before he was rescued.

O'Grady's first task was to make sure he was not captured by the enemy. He **camouflaged** himself with leaves and mud. He also had to be careful about communicating with his base, in case his signals were picked up by the enemy.

Drinking sweat and eating ants

The stranded pilot only had a very limited amount of water. O'Grady drank rainwater and, when this ran out, sucked the sweat from his socks to stay alive. He found what food he could in the **terrain**, including ants.

After six days surviving behind enemy lines, O'Grady was able to make contact with another

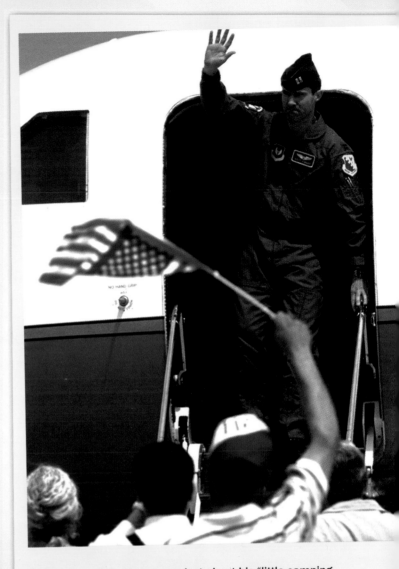

Captain Scott O'Grady was modest about his "little camping trip," saying he had suffered far less than those who were taken prisoner in other conflicts.

F-16 as it flew overhead. Up until then, no one knew if he was dead or alive. Once his position was known, O'Grady was finally rescued by U.S. Marines in helicopters.

Behind enemy lines

The story of Captain O'Grady highlights what soldiers are faced with when they are caught in enemy territory.

Before the mission, a detailed plan will be put together. This will involve as much research as possible into the area. It will also give details of what the survivors will do if things go wrong. Where will he or she move to and what is the plan for rescue? Rescuers will have a copy of this plan. The rescue will be put into action when a mission is completed, when it becomes clear that it is too dangerous to complete it successfully, or when something unexpected happens, as in the case of Captain O'Grady.

The survivor will need the right equipment to survive. Weapons and essential survival equipment such as basic food and water supplies will be attached to clothes or a belt, so that they are never lost. Other items may be needed to cope with extreme conditions, such as spare clothes or sleeping bags. These will be carried in a backpack, but may have to be left aside in a combat situation. If equipment does get lost—as in Captain O'Grady's case—this will make survival more difficult. The survivor may have to rely more on food and other items that can be found in the area.

Avoiding detection

Survivors normally travel at night, when it is easiest to avoid detection. They must not leave tracks. During daylight, survivors can watch the enemy and assess escape routes. The best way to stay hidden is to stay still.

Walking along the bed of a stream is one way to avoid leaving tracks.

Captain O'Grady knew to camouflage himself with leaves and mud. Camouflage should be adjusted when landscape or plant life changes. Strong scents, such as food or soap, can also be dangerous, particularly if the enemy is using tracker dogs. But camouflage does not just mean blending in with trees or the landscape. In areas with lots of people, it can mean blending in by wearing local dress or concealing weapons or objects that would draw attention.

It is important not to be exposed as a shadow, which can happen at dawn or dusk. Shadows of other objects and trees can be used to provide cover when crossing roads. Soldiers also avoid leaving footprints, which can give away the direction of travel.

Search and rescue

Even with the best-planned missions, things can go wrong. Aircraft can crash or be shot down by the enemy, as in the case of Captain O'Grady. Troops on the ground can get separated from their units while avoiding enemy attack or due to extreme weather conditions. When this happens, a search and rescue mission has to be organized.

Soldiers in need of rescuing cannot always openly try to get the attention of rescue teams. This is because they do not want the enemy to spot them as well. If survivors are in **hostile** territory, they need to find the best way of signaling without alerting the enemy, as Captain O'Grady did. Before signaling, the survivors need to have a clear idea of enemy positions. They can then find a place to signal that is not easily visible, such as on the opposite side of a mountain from an enemy base. If signaling from an open space, they need to start by making sure that there are plenty of hiding places and escape routes.

But if there is no danger from the enemy, survivors can find the highest open space and signal openly. Lighting a fire is a good signal, as it can be seen both by day and night. The survivor might also be able to signal by cell phone or radio.

Search and rescue techniques

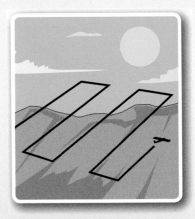

An aerial search will aim to cover the known path of an aircraft or other mission. An airplane flies back and forth in a parallel path across or along the route.

If the search is centered on a particular position, aircraft will search an expanding area around the last known position.

Mountain searches will follow the curves of a mountain, to allow a thorough search. During steep valley searches, the searchers should go back and forth along the valley.

Smoke flares are a good way to attract attention in daylight. However, to minimize the danger of alerting the enemy, flares should be used as close to the time of rescue as possible.

Radio and GPS

Today's soldiers have secure radios to signal for help. They also have **Global Positioning Systems (GPS)** and automatic locator beacons that transmit their exact position to rescuers. However, if these devices get lost or stop working, survivors will fall back on other means of signaling. If nothing else is available, a mirror or any piece of shiny metal can be used to reflect the sun's rays. A signal on the ground can also be made out of natural materials such as branches or rocks.

BENEATH THE WAVES

The U-boat was a key weapon for the German navy in both World War I and World War II. Around two out of three crewmen who served in U-boats were killed.

Survival at sea presents a whole new set of problems. Those who have fought on ships and submarines have to deal with a new enemy—the sea itself. If disaster strikes a submarine, survivors can quickly run out of air, the biggest survival essential of all.

In March 1960, **Soviet** sailor Chayim Sheynin was training in a submarine. Suddenly, it sank 275 meters (900 feet) to the bottom of the Barents Sea. The accident was probably due to a **torpedo** (missile) exploding in the submarine's firing tube.

It was unlikely that anyone would survive. But the crew members put on protective suits and masks with oxygen, the gas humans need to breathe. Each man had to take a turn entering an empty tube normally used to fire torpedoes. The tube was then filled with water at around the same pressure as the sea outside (see Survival Science box). When the men exited the tube into the seawater, they would then climb a cable that, with the help of corks, led to the surface of the water. The men had to climb slowly because of the effect of the change in pressure.

Sheynin suffered a ruptured lung, due to the pressure, but he made it to the surface. He was eventually rescued from the icy water. He never saw any of his crewmates again, although he was told they had survived. He spent three months in a **decompression** chamber, which slowly helped his damaged lung to recover.

SURVIVAL SCIENCE:

The bends
Under deep water, pressure is much higher than it is at the surface. The human body is very sensitive to changes in pressure. When surrounding pressure changes too quickly, nitrogen bubbles can form in the blood. This is called decompression sickness, or "the bends." To prevent this, divers must return to the surface slowly, giving their bodies time to adjust. Decompression sickness is normally treatable, but it can cause paralysis (the inability to move), or even death in extreme cases.

CAPTURE AND ESCAPE

Sometimes survivors are not able to avoid the enemy and are taken into captivity. The Geneva Conventions guarantee the rights of prisoners of war (see the box below). Prisoners of war must not be treated as criminals and should receive adequate food, clothing, and shelter.

The Great Escape

Prisoners of war have a duty to try to escape captivity. One of the most daring escape attempts took place at Stalag Luft III, a German prisoner of war camp in Poland, during World War II. The camp was thought to be escape-proof. Many British and U.S. prisoners were held there specifically because they had already escaped from other camps.

The prisoners formed an escape committee to plan a daring mass-escape. They decided to dig three tunnels, code-named "Tom," "Dick," and "Harry." That way, they would have other options if one tunnel was discovered. The prisoners used boards from their beds to support the tunnels. The main problem was disposing of the dirt that was dug out of the tunnels. The prisoners found ways to hide dirt around the camp. One tunnel, "Tom," was discovered, but eventually "Harry" was completed.

The escape was planned for the moonless night of March 24, 1944. About 200 prisoners were planning to crawl through the tunnel. As the escape began, a problem was discovered. The tunnel did not quite reach the woods outside the camp. When 76 men had escaped, a guard discovered what was happening. Of the 76 men who reached the end of the tunnel, 73 were recaptured. Fifty of these recaptured soldiers were executed. But three men made it to safety. They used **civilian** clothes, maps, and false papers made in the camp to find their way across enemy territory.

HOW SHOULD PRISONERS OF WAR BEHAVE?

The Geneva Conventions are a series of agreements between countries about how prisoners of war must be treated. According to the Geneva Conventions, prisoners of war are only required to give their name, rank, and serial number. But captors will look for signs of prisoners who can provide **intelligence**. Prisoners should try to go as unnoticed as possible, so that they are not identified as possible sources of information.

Prisoners of war at Stalag Luft III in 1943. The prisoners had to appear totally normal to their guards, while planning the daring escape.

Surviving in captivity

Compared to other twentieth century wars, there were relatively few prisoners of war during the Vietnam War (1955–75). However, U.S. prisoners of war in Vietnam often suffered very harsh conditions. John McCain was a U.S. Navy pilot. In 1967 he was shot down near Hanoi, the capital of Vietnam. McCain broke both his arms and his knee as he ejected from his aircraft. He parachuted into a lake and was attacked by an angry mob. He was then taken to the notorious "Hanoi Hilton" prisoner of war camp.

McCain's captors soon discovered that his father was an admiral, a high-ranking official in the U.S. Navy. Knowing they had a high-value prisoner, they offered McCain his freedom—in hopes of a valuable exchange. He refused, honoring the rule that those who were captured first should be released first. McCain spent more than five years as a prisoner, before being finally released in 1973.

"I used to tell movies two or three nights a week. . . . I could recall incredible details. So everybody would come and I might take one full hour describing a movie. . . . We also made fun of the guards. If you don't look out your captors become bigger than life because they have so much control over you." —John McCain

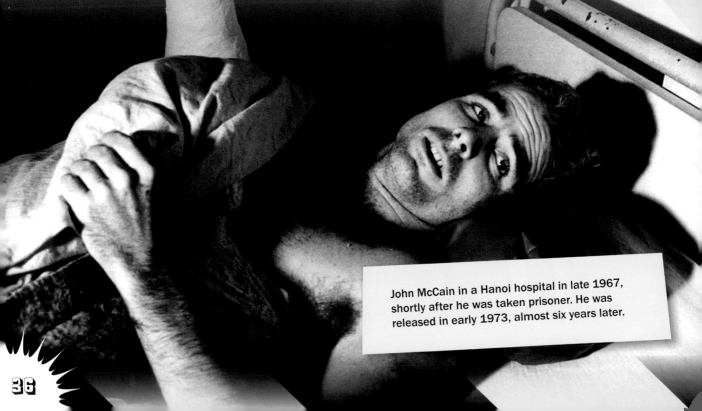

John McCain in a Hanoi hospital in late 1967, shortly after he was taken prisoner. He was released in early 1973, almost six years later.

McCain suffered badly for his decision to refuse release. He was regularly beaten and forced to confess to crimes he did not commit. This shows the stress that even the toughest prisoners can experience.

U.S. MILITARY CODE OF CONDUCT

During the Korean War (1950–53), some prisoners of war were misled into giving away important intelligence. As result, the U.S. Military Code of Conduct was introduced. It says, in part:

If I become a prisoner of war, I will keep faith with my fellow prisoners. I will give no information or take part in any action that will be harmful to my comrades. If I am senior, I will take command. If not, I will obey the lawful orders of those appointed over me and will back them up in every way.

The jungle **terrain** in Sierra Leone provided cover for the daring rescue of Operation Barras. However, the enemy knew the terrain much better than the rescuers. Finding out as much as possible about the area was essential.

Rescue in Sierra Leone

Rescuing captives is difficult and dangerous. Rescuers need to prepare every detail to ensure that the captives are not harmed in the rescue. In August 2000, 11 members of the British Royal Irish Regiment and a local guide were taken prisoner by rebels in Sierra Leone, in Africa. The soldiers were there as part of a **United Nations** force meant to keep peace. The West Side Boys—the group of local rebels holding the soldiers—were unpredictable. So, while the United Nations forces tried to get the men released peacefully, the decision was taken to plan a rescue.

A rescue force was made up of Special Air Service (SAS) and Special Boat Service (SBS) **special forces**, supported by the Parachute Regiment, a group of soldiers specially trained to go behind enemy lines. The rescuers needed to gather as much intelligence as possible. They studied the layout of the two villages the rebels occupied: Gberi Bana, where the captives were held, and Magbeni (see the map at right).

Two four-man special forces units were inserted close to the villages. They managed to get messages to the **hostages**. One of the hostages was able to get a map smuggled out. Concealed inside the top of a pen, the map showed exactly where the hostages were being held. On September 9, the order was given to rescue the captives, in what was known as Operation Barras.

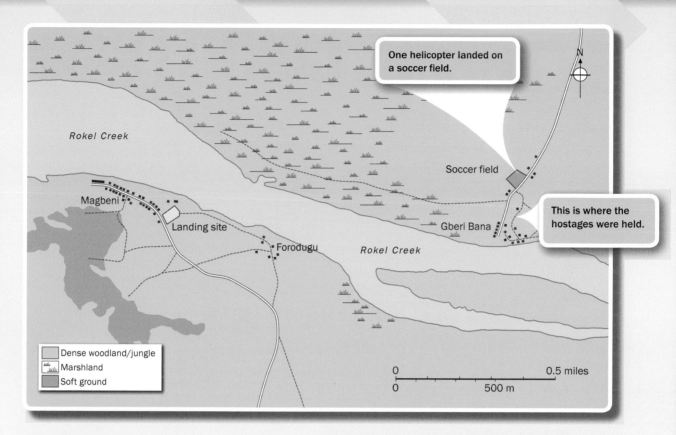

One helicopter landed on a soccer field.

Rokel Creek

Soccer field

This is where the hostages were held.

Magbeni

Landing site

Forodugu

Gberi Bana

Rokel Creek

Dense woodland/jungle
Marshland
Soft ground

| 0 | | 0.5 miles |
| 0 | 500 m | |

The rescue

At 6:16 a.m. the following day, a fleet of helicopters flew low along the river toward the target villages. Trees along the river muffled the noise. One helicopter hovered near the hut where the hostages were being held, while the rescue team slid to the ground on ropes. SAS troops already on the ground and some from a second helicopter landed and distracted the West Side Boys. The hostages were able to walk to their rescue helicopter. A third helicopter had landed at Magbeni to prevent any support for the enemy in Gberi Bana. One SAS trooper was killed in the operation.

Two of the essentials of military survival, detailed planning and grueling training, had paid off. Operation Barras was a success.

CROSSING THE LINES

Crossing back into friendly territory is one of the most dangerous parts of any escape. Borders are always closely watched, and survivors need to be aware of potential obstacles such as barbed wire or **minefields**.

EXTREME CONDITIONS

Many recent conflicts have been fought in extreme **climates** and **terrains**. Troops from North America and Europe have been fighting in the hot deserts of Iraq and the high mountains and extreme temperatures of Afghanistan.

Cold weather survival

Cold weather survival skills are important in extremely cold climates. But they are also important in mountains and even deserts, where temperatures can drop well below freezing at night.

DEALING WITH EXTREME COLD

The biggest risk in extreme cold is **hypothermia**. This happens when the body's temperature falls too low. In the most serious cases, this can lead to death, as seen in the Bravo Two Zero ordeal (see pages 16 and 17). **Frostbite** can also occur at temperatures below 0°C (32°F) and in particularly high winds. Exposed skin can freeze, and long exposure can cause permanent damage. To prevent frostbite, soldiers ensure that their skin is kept covered and warm, particularly their fingers and toes.

Soldiers must carry cold-weather clothing. The head should be covered at all times to prevent heat from escaping there. Clothing should be kept clean and dry, as dirty, damp clothing is less effective at conserving heat. Several layers of clothing are also good, as warm air will be trapped between each layer.

Mountain warfare

Soldiers have often relied on their mountain survival skills in the recent conflict in Afghanistan. Four-fifths of the country is mountainous, with the giant mountains of the Hindu Kush running along the border with Pakistan. The **terrorist** leader Osama bin Laden is thought to be hiding in this wild country.

Mountains present many survival challenges. Mountain peaks are often extremely cold and covered in snow and ice. These high peaks usually have little or no plant life or water. It is also difficult for soldiers to find cover on exposed, rocky slopes. Soldiers may have to move to lower levels to find food and water, or they might rely on extra supplies. Rock-climbing skills are very important.

BUILD AN IGLOO!

1. Cut blocks of frozen snow and create the circular base of the igloo. Make sure to leave enough room inside for yourself and your companions.

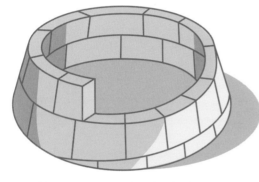

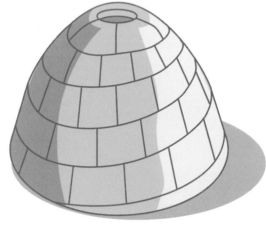

2. Continue to build in a spiral pattern. To create a dome shape, cut blocks with angled bottoms to make each row begin slanting toward the center. You can leave a hole at the top for air circulation, or plug it and create small holes in other places to let air in.

3. Build an entrance to the igloo by digging down and under a small portion of the wall. Then dig back up into the inside of the igloo.

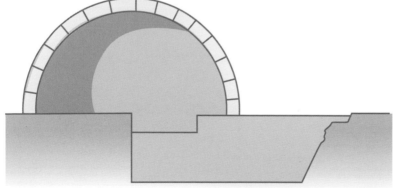

In extremely cold or mountain conditions, there will be few materials to build a shelter. An igloo can be built by cutting blocks of frozen snow.

Desert warfare

There are many obstacles to survival in the desert. Extreme heat can cause sunburn and sunstroke, especially if shade is difficult to find. Deserts often provide few chances for soldiers to conceal themselves from the enemy. One of the main threats to survival in the desert is lack of water. The body also loses fluid very quickly by sweating in the desert heat. Soldiers need to carry lots of bulky water supplies.

An exercise that took place in the hot climate of Kenya, in Africa, shows the importance of water. Small groups of British **recruits** had to **navigate** their way to checkpoints, where they were each given about 250 milliliters (half a pint) of water. After three days, the heat, fatigue, and lack of water was starting to affect the recruits. One recruit grabbed the canister that contained the only water supply, drinking some and spilling more. The exercise became a survival situation, as there was not enough water for 30 recruits and the nearest source was three days away. The strongest recruits were sent for help, and strict **rationing** saved the lives of all of them. This exercise shows the importance of rationing when water is not easily available.

Cover can be very difficult to find in the desert, where there are few plants, trees, and other places to hide. In combat situations soldiers will try to sleep or build shelters behind rocks and in holes in the ground to avoid being seen.

SURVIVAL SCIENCE:

Dehydration

While the human body can survive without food for many days, it can only survive without water for about three days. Apart from air to breathe, water to drink is the most important thing the body needs to survive.

We lose water all the time, even when breathing. Physical activity increases the rate of water loss. The average adult male body contains about 50 liters (11 gallons) of water. Some signs of **dehydration** (lack of water), such as nausea and flushed skin, will be felt if 2 liters (about 4 pints) of water are lost. Survival is unlikely if more than 10 liters (21 pints) are lost.

MAKING A SOLAR STILL

Even when a soldier is caught in the driest desert, there is a way to get water. By making a solar still, people can use the power of the sun to collect water. Dig a depression in the ground. Weigh down a sheet of plastic with stones to form a cone shape in the ground. Place a can or cup at the base of the cone to collect water, and run a tube from the inside of the can to the surface. The sun will heat the air and ground below the sheet to release water vapor (gas). When the plastic cools at night, the vapor will become liquid water and collect in the cup. Use the tube to suck water from the can. This works well in deserts with hot days and cold nights.

THE HOME FRONT

*Most of the survival stories in this book are about soldiers who put themselves in harm's way. But many of the **casualties** of war since 1900 have been ordinary **civilians**, caught up in devastating conflicts and bombings.*

The Blitz

During World War II, both sides bombed enemy cities to damage the spirit of the people. When the war began in 1939, civilians were issued gas masks in case of attack by poisonous gas—although such attacks did not happen. Many children were **evacuated** from vulnerable cities.

In September 1940, the bombing of British cities that became known as "the Blitz" began. Night after night, air-raid sirens would signal a new bombing raid. Air-raid officials were responsible for organizing and protecting people during these air raids. There are many amazing tales of courage.

A 14-year-old boy from London joined the local air-raid office as a messenger. One night, a phosphorus bomb fell through the roof of a house, coming to rest beneath the floorboards. Phosphorus burns fiercely and brightly, so this bomb was designed to start fires. The bomb needed to be kept in water to prevent it from igniting. The young messenger was the only member of the unit small enough to crawl through the tunnel made by the bomb and pour water on it. He did this twice a day, until it was made safe by a bomb disposal team a week later. His courage, and that of many others, saved many lives during the Blitz.

WORLD WAR II SURVIVAL

Millions of people around the world were killed during World War II. At least six million Jews were murdered by the German Nazis in the Holocaust. There is not space in this book to tell the many tales of heroism of those who survived the Holocaust. If you are interested in finding out more about the courage of ordinary people caught up in the horrors of war, your local library is a great place to find out more.

In the United Kingdom, many people built Anderson shelters in their backyards during World War II. These cramped iron shelters were safer than staying in their houses.

Civilian survival

Recent wars have had just as big an impact on civilians. Since 2003, more than 100,000 civilians have died in the Iraq conflict. Since the 1980s, the people of Afghanistan have endured various wars almost constantly.

Daily survival in Iraq

Ever since the U.S.-led invasion in 2003, conflict has affected daily life in Iraq. Some Iraqis who opposed the invasion continue to attack troops. Their bombs and explosives are often just as likely to kill and injure civilians as soldiers. For people living in Iraq's capital, Baghdad, things have become so dangerous that many children have sometimes stopped going to school, and even shopping for food has been difficult.

Buildings in Iraq were bombed at the start of the U.S.-led war. The continuing conflict has destroyed many more buildings since then.

Dangers in Afghanistan

In 2009, a report by the **United Nations** said that civilian deaths were increasing in Afghanistan. Most were caused by **IEDs** planted by forces that opposed the presence of the United States and the U.S.-supported Afghan government. However, there was also a significant risk from air strikes by the United States, United Kingdom, and the other countries working with them. The United Nations is working to clear **minefields** and other explosives, as well as educating civilians about the dangers.

LANDMINES

Landmines are explosives hidden beneath the ground. They are one of the greatest dangers that civilians face in many countries around the world. Wherever there is conflict, landmines are buried. Then, once the conflict is over, they remain a deadly problem for the civilian population. Landmines are designed to cause serious injury or death by exploding when pressure is put on them—for example, by someone stepping on them. More than 150 countries around the world have now banned landmines completely, including Australia, Germany, and the United Kingdom.

A worker in Cambodia searches for landmines with a metal detector. Clearing landmines is slow, difficult, and dangerous work.

Living with war means that civilians in Iraq and Afghanistan deal with constant dangers. As a result, they do not have many of the freedoms that we take for granted. The risk of minefields and bombs means that travel is very difficult. Fear of explosives also stops land from being used for farming, which can lead to food shortages. Those of us who do not live in these conditions can only imagine what this daily battle for survival is like.

HOW WOULD YOU SURVIVE?

Our armed forces have to survive not only in the toughest locations but also against enemy forces in order to protect all of us.

*In this book, you have been able to read some amazing stories of military survival, from highly trained **special forces** soldiers surviving against the odds to **civilians** with no military training but an overwhelming will to live. All of these people share some common qualities, which can give us an idea about what it takes to survive.*

Planning

Planning is often the key to survival, from the most basic level of making sure that someone is aware of your likely location, to the detailed planning that enabled the rescue of **hostages** in Sierra Leone. Planning means having the right information and equipment to be prepared for anything that the **terrain**, or the enemy, may throw at you. Extreme conditions, particularly in conflict zones, are unpredictable. Soldiers need to be able to adapt.

Training and fitness

In many of the stories in this book, soldiers have survived because of their training. They are physically fit and mentally strong enough to cope with extreme conditions, but also trained in the techniques needed to survive when their backs are against the wall.

Courage

Planning and physical fitness can be learned as part of military training. But many of the people in this book who survived extraordinary situations also demonstrate qualities that are more difficult to teach. There are amazing tales of courage from those who stormed the beaches at D-Day, were captured by the enemy, or just tried to live their everyday lives in the middle of a conflict.

Do you have what it takes?

Can you think of other qualities that helped these people to survive? Do you think you have what it takes to survive when doing so seems to be impossible?

Many of these qualities are important in everyday life, as well as in the military. Planning and preparation are important whether you are completing a school project or going on a camping trip. Getting plenty of exercise and keeping your body healthy will help you at school and at home, as well as in a survival situation. We all sometimes need courage to complete a difficult task, and a bit of luck, too—although we hope we will never have to face some of the life or death situations described in this book.

SURVIVAL ESSENTIALS

SURVIVAL KIT

Anyone trying to survive in the wilderness should have a basic survival kit. This will vary depending on the **terrain**. The following are the major needs you will have, and the materials you will need to meet those needs. Some equipment will have multiple uses:

Fire
To light fires, you will need matches (waterproof if possible), a candle, or a small lens for focusing the sun's rays.

Water
You will need water purification tablets and materials to store water.

Signaling and navigation
In order to get rescuers' attention, you will need a mirror, to create a reflection. To find your way, you will need a compass.

Food
To find and prepare food, you will need a fishing line and hook, snare wire, and a knife.

Shelter
An emergency blanket, also called a space blanket or solar blanket, will give you shelter in an emergency situation. The blanket is made of a thin sheet of plastic coated with a metallic material. It is useful in survival situations because it is lightweight and waterproof, and it does a good job of holding heat in.

First aid
In case of injury, you will need a first-aid kit that includes bandages in a range of sizes to protect small wounds and blisters, bandages for covering larger wounds and keeping broken limbs in place, **antiseptic** cream and wipes, gauze padding to soak up blood and keep wounds clean, and painkillers.

SURVIVAL MANUAL

The U.S. Army Survival Manual outlines a plan for survival based on the letters in the word *survival*. (The following headings are taken from the survival manual, but the descriptions are not.)

S: Size up the situation
Conceal yourself from the enemy and take time to think about your options for survival. What are the surroundings like? What is the enemy doing? Consider your own physical condition, whether you are injured, and what equipment you have. In making your survival plan, you need to consider your own physical needs for food, water, and more.

U: Use all senses, Undue haste makes waste
Use all your senses before deciding what to do. Don't rush into any decisions or situations that might put you in danger.

R: Remember where you are
You need to always know where you are and relate it to maps and compasses. Make sure you know where you are in relation to the enemy, as well as in relation to friendly areas. Locate the nearest sources of water and shelter.

V: Vanquish fear and panic
Vanquish means to defeat something totally. So, to vanquish fear and panic, you need to remain calm. Fear and panic can cause you to lose energy and make bad decisions.

I: Improvise
Make the best use of the materials available to you, either in your survival kit or in the natural materials found in the environment.

V: Value living
We have become used to a soft life. In a survival situation, we need to show a will to live and a refusal to give in, no matter the obstacles.

A: Act like the natives
People and animals have adapted to their environment. Watch what the local people do and use this knowledge to guide your own actions. For example, when and where do they eat and get water?

L: Live by your wits, but for now, Learn basic skills
Without basic survival skills, your chances of surviving an **evasion** and escape situation are slight. Learn survival skills and use your best instincts.

GLOSSARY

altitude height above sea level. The peaks of mountains can be thousands of feet above sea level.

antiseptic anything that prevents the growth of the tiny living things that cause disease

camouflage use of colors and patterns to blend in with natural surroundings. Many animals have natural camouflage. Humans use patterned clothes and other materials to camouflage themselves.

captivity being forcibly held somewhere

casualty someone who is killed, injured, captured, or missing, particularly in a military conflict

civilian anyone who is not a member of the armed forces

climate weather patterns in an area

constellation group of stars

decompression when people have been subjected to high pressure, such as being underwater, the pressure needs to be released gradually to avoid injury. This can be controlled in a decompression chamber.

dehydration when the body suffers from lack of water. This happens when the body uses more water than it takes in.

elite group selected from a larger group. Elite forces are selected to be the best and most highly trained soldiers for difficult missions.

embassy official headquarters for a country located within a foreign country

endurance ability to deal with challenges

evacuate leave or ask people to leave an area until danger has passed

evasion avoiding something, such as being captured

frostbite injury or destruction of the skin and tissue underneath that results from continued exposure to freezing temperatures

g-force object's acceleration relative to the force of gravity that pulls us all toward Earth's surface (g). Jet-fighter pilots experience forces much greater than gravity.

Global Positioning System (GPS) device that uses satellite signals to pinpoint the user's exact position on Earth's surface

gravity force exerted by large bodies such as Earth. Gravity holds us onto the surface of Earth. Gravity is weaker in space.

guerrilla any group engaging in irregular fighting, usually against a larger force or invading army

hostage someone who is captured and used as a way of bargaining by his or her captors

hostile not friendly or welcoming, and possibly aggressive

hypothermia condition in which the body loses heat from its core. If untreated, big drops in the body's temperature can cause death.

Improvised Explosive Device (IED) crude bomb made with everyday materials and a detonator

intelligence in the military, intelligence is knowledge that can be useful—for example, details of enemy troops

minefield area where explosive mines are placed to cause casualties or to prevent the area from being crossed

navigate find the way to where you want to travel

ration to limit the supply of something, particularly food. If you know that food needs to last for many days, the supply for each day will be limited to make the food last longer.

recruit someone who recently joined the military

SERE training training in Survival, Evasion, Resistance, and Escape for military personnel who are at risk of being captured by an enemy

Soviet from the Soviet Union, a group of countries, including the present-day Russian Federation, that existed from 1922 to 1991

special forces groups, normally selected from the regular armed forces, that are used to carry out particularly skilled or dangerous missions, such as working behind enemy lines

terrain area of land, particularly relating to the landforms and other features of the land—for example, mountain or desert terrain

terrorist anyone who seeks to achieve political goals by carrying out acts of violence on civilians

torpedo missile fired from a submarine

United Nations organization that includes most countries in the world, it was formed after World War II to manage disputes between different countries and to prevent wars

FIND OUT MORE

BOOKS

Gilpin, Daniel. *Military Vehicles* (*Machines Close-Up* series). New York, NY: Marshall Cavendish Benchmark, 2011.

Grant, R. G. *Warrior: A Visual History of the Fighting Man*. New York, NY: Dorling Kindersley, 2007.

Montana, Jack. *Escape and Evasion* (*Special Forces* series). Broomall, PA: Mason Crest, 2011.

Williams, Brian. *The War in Afghanistan* (*Timelines* series). Mankato, MN: Arcturus, 2011.

Wilson, Patrick. *Survival Equipment* (*Elite Forces Survival Guide* series). Broomall, PA: Mason Crest, 2003.

Wilson, Patrick. *Survival First Aid* (*Elite Forces Survival Guide* series). Broomall, PA: Mason Crest, 2003.

WEBSITES

News websites will give details of specific conflicts. When searching for information on the Internet, always be sure that the website you are using is reliable. Is the information provided by an established or official organization? Is it designed to give a biased (one-sided) view? Here are some other websites to try:

www.army.mil
Visit the official U.S. Army website to learn more about its operations.

www.goarmy.com/special_forces/training.jsp
This U.S. Army website gives more details about its special forces.

www.army.mod.uk
Visit the official British Army website to learn more about its operations.

www.holocaustsurvivors.org
Read stories from those who survived the Holocaust during World War II.

INDEX